Longman Integrated
Comprehension and
Composition Series

Stage 1　Fiction

Fred Smith

Brian Richards

Longman

1 That's Fred Smith

Mr Jones is standing at his window.
   His mother is sitting near the fire. She is reading a book. 'What are you looking at?' she asks her son.
   'I'm looking at a boy,' Mr Jones answers. 'He's near our
5 wall. He's looking at our apple tree.'
   'Ah,' his mother says. 'Ah. What's he doing now?'
   'He's coming over our wall now. He's a fat boy. He has big ears and a long red nose.'
   'And what's he doing now?'
10 'He's taking an apple. Now he's eating it.'
   'Ah,' Mr Jones's mother says. 'That's Fred Smith.'

GUIDED COMPOSITION

Answer these questions in one paragraph. Do not use more than 50 words.

1 Is Mr Jones standing at his door or at his window?
2 What is he looking at?
3 Is the boy fat or thin?
4 Has he small ears and a short nose or big ears and a long nose?
5 Is he taking an apple from Mr Jones's tree or not?
6 What's he doing with the apple now?
7 Is the boy's name Fred Smith or not?

MULTIPLE CHOICE QUESTIONS

Only one answer is right in each exercise. Choose (a), (b), (c) or (d). Then look at the text.

1 Mr Jones ...
   (a) is eating breakfast.
   (b) is reading.
   (c) is standing at a window.
   (d) has a big nose.

2 One of these is near the wall ...
   (a) the fire.
   (b) Mr Jones's mother.
   (c) Fred Smith.
   (d) Mr Jones.

3 'I'm looking ...... a boy.' (line 4)
   (a) at   (b) to   (c) in   (d) on

4 We have an apple tree. It is ...... apple tree. (l. 5)
   (a) his   (b) their   (c) our   (d) your

5 'What ...... now?' (l. 6)
   (a) he does   (b) is he doing   (c) does he do   (d) he is doing

6 'What are you looking at?' she ...... her son. (l. 3)
   (a) speaks   (b) asks   (c) answers   (d) says

7 'He's coming over our wall now.' (l. 7)
   (a) He's near our wall now.   (b) He's in front of our wall now.
   (c) He's behind our wall now.   (d) He's on our wall now.

8 Mr Jones is Mrs Jones's son. She is his ...... (l. 2)
   (a) mother   (b) daughter   (c) sister   (d) wife

SENTENCE STRUCTURE

Make a sentence from these words; then check your answer against the text.

He nose a long has red.
He .... (line 8)

3

2 Boys are silly

Fred is in his room. He is sitting on his bed. He is eating an apple. It is a nice apple and it comes from Mr Jones's tree.

His sister Jenny comes to the window. 'Hullo, Fred,' she says.

5 Fred jumps. 'Oh!' he says. He puts the apple behind his back.

'What are you doing?' Jenny asks.

'I'm . . . I'm writing a letter,' her brother answers.

'You're not writing a letter,' Jenny says. 'You're eating an
10 apple.'

'No,' Fred says. 'I'm writing a letter. And it says: "Dear Jenny, please go away".'

'Oh, boys!' Jenny says. 'Boys are silly!'

GUIDED COMPOSITION

Answer these questions in one paragraph. Do not use more than 50 words.

1 Is Fred sitting on his bed or not?
2 Is he reading a book or is he eating an apple?
3 Does Jenny come to the window or not?
4 What does Fred do with the apple?
5 What does Jenny ask?
6 What does Fred answer?
7 Does Jenny say, 'You're not writing a letter. You're eating an apple' or not?

MULTIPLE CHOICE QUESTIONS

Only one answer is right in each exercise. Choose (a), (b), (c) or (d).

1 Fred is ...
   (a) in bed.
   (b) at the window.
   (c) on his bed.
   (d) in Mr Jones's apple tree.

2 Fred is ...
   (a) eating an apple.
   (b) writing a letter.
   (c) coming to the window.
   (d) going away.

3 The apple comes ...... Mr Jones's tree. (line 2)
   (a) to   (b) at   (c) by   (d) from

4 Fred puts the apple ...... his back. (ll. 5–6)
   (a) in front of   (b) at   (c) behind   (d) to

5 Fred's letter says, 'Please ...... away.' (l. 12)
   (a) you go   (b) go   (c) going   (d) goes

6 Apples are not ...
   (a) red   (b) blue   (c) yellow   (d) green

7 Jenny is Fred's .... (l. 3)
   (a) son   (b) daughter   (c) sister   (d) mother

8 Fred is Jenny's .... (l. 8)
   (a) father   (b) son   (c) daughter   (d) brother

SENTENCE STRUCTURE

Join these sentences with 'and'; then check your answer against the text.

It is a nice apple. It comes from Mr Jones's tree.

It .... (line 2)

3 A happy family

Bill Smith is Fred and Jenny's father. He is a bus driver. He is happy now. 'We're going out,' he says.

Fred is happy and Jenny is happy, too.

'Can we take your bus?'

5 'Don't be silly,' his father says.

'Can we go to the sea?' Jenny asks.

'That's silly,' Fred says. 'We're going into the country.'

'I'm not,' Jenny says.

'And I'm not going to the sea,' Fred says.

10 'All right,' their father says. 'We're not going into the country.'

'Good,' Jenny says.

'And we're not going to the sea.'

'Good,' Fred says.

15 'We're going into the garden. Good.'

GUIDED COMPOSITION

Answer these questions in one paragraph. Do not use more than 45 words.

1 Is Bill Smith happy or sad?
2 Are he and his children going out or not?
3 Does Jenny say, 'Can we go to the sea?' or not?
4 Does Fred say, 'We're going into the country' or not?
5 Do Bill and his children go into the country or not?
6 Do they go to the sea or not?
7 Do they go out or not?

MULTIPLE CHOICE QUESTIONS

Only one answer is right in each exercise. Choose (a), (b), (c) or (d).

1 Fred says 'Good' because ...
   (a) Jenny can't go to the sea.
   (b) Jenny is going into the country.
   (c) His father is going to take his bus.
   (d) He is going to the sea.

2 (a) The Smiths go into the country.
   (b) The Smiths don't go out.
   (c) The Smiths go to the sea.
   (d) Bill Smith takes his bus.

3 Bill Smith is the father of Fred and Jenny. (line 1)
   (a) Bill Smith is Fred's and Jenny father.
   (b) Bill Smith is Fred and Jenny's father.
   (c) Bill Smith is Fred and Jenny father.
   (d) Bill Smith is Fred's and Jenny's father.

4 Fred says, 'We're going into the country.' (l. 7) Jenny says, '......'
   (a) We go   (b) You are   (c) I'm not   (d) I don't

5 'We're going ...... the garden.' (l. 15)
   (a) on   (b) at   (c) in   (d) into

6 Bill is Jenny's father. She is his .... (l. 1)
   (a) sister   (b) daughter   (c) mother   (d) wife

7 'Can we go to the sea?' Jenny .... (l. 6)
   (a) speaks   (b) questions   (c) asks   (d) answers

8 There are ...... in the sea.
   (a) trees   (b) houses   (c) gardens   (d) fish

SENTENCE STRUCTURE

Make one sentence from these two, using 'and' and 'too'; then check you answer against the text.

Fred is happy. Jenny is happy.

Fred .... (line 3)

4 Tiger—Fred's friend

Fred is in his room. He is doing his homework. 'Homework isn't nice,' he says to Tiger.
   'Tiger is my friend,' he writes. 'He is my cat. He is small and black and his eyes are green. I give him fish and milk.'
5   Tiger looks at Fred.
   'Fish? Milk?' Fred says. 'I can't come now. I can't give you food now, can I? I'm working.'
   He writes: 'He comes to my room and looks at me. And I give him fish and milk.'
10   Tiger says, 'Miaou.'
   'No, Tiger,' Fred says. 'I can't come now. I'm doing my homework.'

GUIDED COMPOSITION

Answer these questions in one paragraph. Do not use more than 50 words.

1 Is Fred in the garden or in his room?
2 What is he doing?
3 Is Tiger Fred's friend or not?
4 What is Tiger?
5 Does Fred write, 'I give him fish and milk,' or not?
6 What does Tiger say to Fred?
7 Does Fred say, 'I can't come now,' or not?
8 Does he give Tiger food now or not?

MULTIPLE CHOICE QUESTIONS

Only one answer is right in each exercise. Choose (a), (b), (c) or (d).

1 (a) Tiger is big and black.
  (b) Fred is Tiger's cat.
  (c) Tiger is Fred's cat.
  (d) Tiger does homework.

2 (a) Tiger doesn't eat.
  (b) Fred eats Tiger.
  (c) Tiger eats Fred.
  (d) Tiger eats fish and milk.

3 Fred is …… his room. (line 1)
  (a) in   (b) to   (c) into   (d) on

4 'I can't give you food now, ……?' (ll. 6–7)
  (a) can't I   (b) do I   (c) can I   (d) am I

5 'He comes …… my room.' (l. 8)
  (a) in   (b) on   (c) at   (d) to

6 He is …… his homework. (l. 1)
  (a) doing   (b) making   (c) taking   (d) answering

7 A cat's eyes are ……. (l. 4)
  (a) brown   (b) black   (c) grey   (d) green

8 'I can't …… you food now.' (ll. 6–7)
  (a) put   (b) eat   (c) give   (d) take

SENTENCE STRUCTURE

Rewrite this sentence; then check your answer against the text.

I give fish and milk to him.

I give him ………………………………………………… (line 4)

5 Tiger's supper

Bill Smith is in his garden. There is a small tree in the garden and Bill is sitting under it. It is evening. Soon he is going to eat his supper.

Fred comes into the garden.

5 'Hullo, Fred,' Bill says to his son. He is happy. 'There's fish for supper.'

'Good,' Fred says.

'Fish is nice,' Bill says. 'And what's Tiger doing now?'

'Oh,' Fred says. 'Tiger's standing on the kitchen table.'

10 'Tiger's on the kitchen table? What's he doing there?'

'He's eating his supper. He's eating fish.'

'Tiger's eating fish!' Bill is not happy now. 'That's not Tiger's supper! That's *my* supper!'

GUIDED COMPOSITION

Answer these questions in one paragraph. Do not use more than 50 words.

1 Is it morning or evening?
2 Is Bill Smith sitting under a tree or not?
3 Is he happy or sad?
4 Is he going to have his breakfast or his supper?
5 What is he going to eat?
6 Is Fred's cat, Tiger, in the kitchen or in the garden?
7 Is he standing on the kitchen table or not?
8 What is he eating?
9 Is he eating his supper or Bill Smith's supper?

MULTIPLE CHOICE QUESTIONS

Only one answer in each exercise is right. Choose (a), (b), (c) or (d).

1 Bill Smith is ...
   (a) in the garden.
   (b) on the kitchen table.
   (c) in his house.
   (d) in his room.

2 Tiger is ...
   (a) eating his supper.
   (b) in the garden.
   (c) eating Bill Smith's supper.
   (d) eating the kitchen table.

3 Bill Smith is sitting ...... the tree. (line 2)
   (a) at   (b) in   (c) under   (d) down

4 Fred comes ...... the garden. (l. 4)
   (a) on   (b) at   (c) into   (d) over

5 'What's Tiger ......?' (l. 8)
   (a) does   (b) doing   (c) do   (d) doesn't

6 There isn't ...... in the kitchen.
   (a) food   (b) water   (c) a table   (d) a tree

7 We eat supper .... (ll. 2–3)
   (a) in the morning   (b) in the evening
   (c) in the garden   (d) in the afternoon

8 We don't eat ....
   (a) food   (b) fish   (c) trees   (d) supper

SENTENCE STRUCTURE

Join these two sentences with 'and'; then check your answer against the text.

There is a small tree. Bill is sitting under the tree.

There is .... (lines 1–2)

6 School is silly, too

Charley is Fred's friend. 'Are you coming to school?' he asks. Charley is tall and thin but Fred is short and fat.

'No,' Fred answers. 'What do we do at school? We sit at silly desks. The silly teacher writes silly things on the blackboard. We write silly things in our books. She asks us silly questions. The lessons are silly. School is silly! No, I'm going for a walk. Are you coming?'

'No, Fred. I'm not,' Charley says. 'Look at the sky! It's going to rain.'

10   The two boys go to school.

GUIDED COMPOSITION

Answer these questions in one paragraph. Do not use more than 45 words.
1 Is Charley Fred's brother or Fred's friend?
2 Is he tall and thin or short and fat?
3 Is he going to school or not?
4 Does Fred say, 'School is silly! I'm going for a walk,' or not?
5 Is Charley going for a walk or not?
6 Does he say, 'It's going to rain' or 'It's a nice day'?
7 Do the two boys go to school or do they go for a walk?

MULTIPLE CHOICE QUESTIONS

Only one answer is right in each exercise. Choose (a), (b), (c) or (d).

1 (a) Charley doesn't go to school.
  (b) Fred doesn't go to school.
  (c) Charley is going to school.
  (d) Fred goes for a walk.

2 (a) Charley is short and fat.
  (b) Charley is tall and fat.
  (c) Charley is short and thin.
  (d) Fred isn't tall and thin.

3 'We sit .... silly desks.' (lines 3–4)
  (a) to   (b) at   (c) in   (d) on

4 'Are you coming?' (l. 8)
  'No, Fred, ...'
  (a) not coming   (b) I am   (c) I don't   (d) I'm not

5 'I'm going ...... a walk.' (ll. 6–7)
  (a) to   (b) at   (c) from   (d) for

6 Charley is thin, but Fred is .... (l. 2)
  (a) tall   (b) thick   (c) fat   (d) long

7 'We .... silly things in our silly books.' (l. 5)
  (a) answer   (b) put   (c) write   (d) do

8 'She ...... us silly questions.' (ll. 5–6)
  (a) says   (b) puts   (c) answers   (d) asks

SENTENCE STRUCTURE

Join these two sentences with 'but'; then check your answer against the text.

Charley is tall and thin. Fred is short and fat.

Charley is .... (line 2)

7 Fred? He's a good boy

Miss Murch says, 'Good morning, girls and boys.'
'Good morning, Miss Murch,' the children answer.
'This is for you, Miss Murch,' Fred says. He gives Miss Murch an apple.
'Thank you, Fred,' Miss Murch says. 'This is a nice red apple.'
'The blackboard isn't clean,' Fred says. 'Can I clean it for you?' He cleans it.
'Thank you, Fred,' Miss Murch says. 'You're a good boy.'
'Yes, Miss Murch. I'm a good boy,' Fred says.
Miss Murch writes on the blackboard.
Fred goes to his desk. He sits beside Charley. He opens his book.
Charley does not speak to him.

GUIDED COMPOSITION

Answer these questions in one paragraph. Do not use more than 50 words.

1 Are the children at school or not?
2 What is their teacher's name?
3 What does Fred give her?
4 What does she say?
5 Does Fred say, 'The blackboard isn't clean' or not?
6 What does he do to the blackboard?
7 Does the teacher say, 'You're a good boy' or not?
8 Does Fred sit beside Charley or behind Charley?
9 Does Charley speak to him or not?

MULTIPLE CHOICE QUESTIONS

Only one answer is right in each exercise. Choose (a), (b), (c) or (d).

1 Fred ...
   (a) cleans the blackboard.
   (b) gives Miss Murch to an apple.
   (c) cleans his desk.
   (d) cleans the apple.

2 Charley ...
   (a) sits near Miss Murch.
   (b) sits near the blackboard.
   (c) sits near Fred.
   (d) sits in front of Fred.

3 'This is ...... you, Miss Murch,' Fred says. (line 3)
   (a) to   (b) for   (c) on   (d) from

4 Miss Murch writes ...... the blackboard. (l. 11)
   (a) in   (b) at   (c) to   (d) on

5 Fred goes ...... his desk. (l. 12)
   (a) on   (b) in   (c) into   (d) to

6 'Good morning, Miss Murch,' the children .... (l. 2)
   (a) ask   (b) speak   (c) answer   (d) question

7 There isn't ...... in Fred's classroom.
   (a) chalk   (b) paper   (c) rain   (d) a desk

8 Charley does not ...... to him. (l. 14)
   (a) ask   (b) answer   (c) say   (d) speak

SENTENCE STRUCTURE

Rewrite this sentence; then check your answer against the text.

He gives an apple to Miss Murch.

He gives .... (lines 3–4)

8 Fred writes a composition

'Write a composition,' Miss Murch says. 'Its title is "My Friend".'

'He is a boy,' Fred writes. 'He is thin. He has long legs and long arms. He is in this class. He sits between me and the wall.'

5　　He looks at Charley.

'His face isn't clean. He has a small head but I haven't. I have a big head.

'Mr Jones is not my friend. His apples are good.

'Mr Jones is Miss Murch's friend. He takes her hand. He
10　says, "Oh, Mildred".

'My friend doesn't take my hand and he doesn't say, "Oh, Fred".

'My friend's hands aren't clean.'

GUIDED COMPOSITION

Answer these questions in one paragraph. Do not use more than 50 words.

1　Is Fred writing a composition or a letter?
2　What is its title?
3　Does Fred's friend sit beside him or in front of him?
4　What is his name?
5　Is Mr Jones Fred's friend or not?
6　Is he Miss Murch's friend or not?
7　What does he do to Miss Murch's hand?
8　What does he say to her?
9　Does Fred's friend do this?
10　Are his hands clean or not?

MULTIPLE CHOICE QUESTIONS

Only one answer is right in each exercise. Choose (a), (b), (c) or (d).

1 Fred's friend is ...
   (a) Miss Murch.
   (b) Charley.
   (c) Mr Jones.
   (d) Mildred.

2 (a) Charley has long legs and short arms.
   (b) Fred has long legs and long arms.
   (c) Charley has long legs and long arms.
   (d) Charley has short legs and long arms.

3 Fred is writing a composition. ...... title is 'My Friend.' (lines 1–2)
   (a) His   (b) It's   (c) My   (d) Its

4 'He has a small head but I ......' (l. 6)
   (a) have   (b) don't have   (c) haven't   (d) do

5 'Mr Jones is Miss Murch's friend. He takes ...... hand.' (l. 9)
   (a) his   (b) your   (c) my   (d) her

6 The opposite of long is ...
   (a) little   (b) short   (c) tall   (d) small

7 Charley sits between Fred and the wall.   (l. 4)
   (a) The wall—Fred—Charley   (b) Fred—Charley—the wall
   (c) Charley—Fred—the wall   (d) Charley—the wall—Fred

8 Mr Jones is Miss Murch's ...   (l. 9)
   (a) sister   (b) friend   (c) brother   (d) father

SENTENCE STRUCTURE

Join these two sentences with 'and'; then check your answer against the text.

He has long legs. He has long arms.

He has .... (lines 3–4)

9 Miss Murch's face is red

'Shut your books,' Miss Murch says. 'You can go now.'
'Come on, Fred,' Charley says and stands up.
But Fred is looking out of the window.
'You can go now,' Miss Murch says. 'What are you doing,
5 Fred?'
'I'm looking out of the window, Miss Murch,' Fred answers.
'I'm looking at Mr Jones. Mr Jones is standing in the road.
He's looking at his watch.'
'You can go now, Fred,' Miss Murch says.
10 'Mr Jones is nice,' Fred says. 'And, oh, your face is red, Miss
Murch.'
Miss Murch says, 'Oh!'
'His first name's Harold,' Fred says to Charley.

GUIDED COMPOSITION

Answer these questions in one paragraph. Do not use more than 55 words.

1 Does Miss Murch say, 'Shut your books' or 'Open your books'?
2 Does she ask Fred, 'What are you doing?' or not?
3 Does Fred answer, 'I'm looking out of the window' or not?
4 What is he looking at?
5 Is Mr Jones standing in the road or not?
6 What is he looking at?
7 Does Fred say, 'Your face is red, Miss Murch' or not?
8 What does Miss Murch say?

MULTIPLE CHOICE QUESTIONS

Only one answer is right in each exercise. Choose (a), (b), (c) or (d).

1 (a) Charley is looking out of the window.
  (b) Mr Jones is looking out of the window.
  (c) Fred is looking out of the window.
  (d) Miss Murch is looking out of the window.

2 (a) Charley's first name is Harold.
  (b) Miss Murch's first name is Harold.
  (c) Fred's first name is Harold.
  (d) Mr Jones's first name is Harold.

3 'You can ...... now.' (line 1)
  (a) go (b) to go (c) going (d) goes

4 'Come......, Fred.' (l. 2)
  (a) at (b) to (c) on (d) for

5 'Mr Jones is standing .... the road.' (l. 7)
  (a) at (b) to (c) into (d) in

6 Don't open your books. ...... them. (l. 1)
  (a) Put (b) Read (c) Take (d) Shut

7 'What are you doing, Fred?' (l. 6)
  'I'm looking out of the window,' he ....
  (a) speaks (b) answers (c) questions (d) asks

8 One of these is a first name:
  (a) bird (b) Mary (c) wall (d) watch

SENTENCE STRUCTURE

Join these two sentences with 'and'; then check your answer against the text.

'Come on, Fred,' Charley says. He stands up.

'Come on, ... (line 2)

10 Mildred is a nice name

Mr Jones's mother is reading. She shuts her book and puts it down. 'What are you doing, Harold?' she asks.
   Her son is in the kitchen. 'I'm cleaning my shoes,' he says. 'Ah.'
5   Harold comes into the room. 'All right?'
   'Oh yes. Clean shoes. Clean shirt. And the trousers are new. Are you going out?'
   'Er, yes, I am.'
   'Ah. She's a nice girl, Harold. What's her first name?'
10   'Her first name?'
   'Miss Murch's first name. You're going out with her.'
   'Oh.' Mr Jones looks at his shoes. 'Mildred,' he says.
   'Ah,' Mrs Jones says. 'It's a nice name.'

GUIDED COMPOSITION

Answer these questions in one paragraph. Do not use more than 50 words.

1 What is Mr Jones's mother doing?
2 What does she do with her book?
3 Does she speak to her son or not?
4 What is he doing?
5 Is he going out or not?
6 Is he going out with his mother or not?
7 Is he going out with a nice girl or not?
8 What is her name?

MULTIPLE CHOICE QUESTIONS

Only one answer is right in each exercise. Choose (a), (b), (c) or (d).

1 (a) Mrs Jones puts the shoes down.
  (b) Harold puts the book down.
  (c) Mrs Jones puts the book down.
  (d) Harold puts his shoes down.

2 (a) Mrs Jones is cleaning Harold's trousers.
  (b) Harold is cleaning his trousers.
  (c) Mrs Jones is cleaning Harold's shirt.
  (d) Harold is cleaning his shoes.

3 'Are you going out?' (line 7)
  (a) 'Yes, going.'   (b) 'Yes, I am.'   (c) 'Yes, I go.'   (d) 'Yes, I do.'

4 'And the trousers ...... new.' (l. 6)
  (a) is   (b) is going to be   (c) isn't   (d) are

5 'You're going out ...... her.' (l. 11)
  (a) with   (b) at   (c) from   (d) behind

6 The opposite of 'down' is ...
  (a) in   (b) up   (c) from   (d) near

7 Mr Jones ...... his shoes. (l. 12)
  (a) looks at   (b) gives   (c) looks   (d) puts

8 Harold doesn't have
  (a) a hat   (b) a dress   (c) a coat   (d) a suit

SENTENCE STRUCTURE

Join these two sentences with 'and'; then check your answer against the text.

She shuts her book. She puts her book down.

She shuts .... (lines 1–2)

11 Breakfast? No thank you!

The title of the composition is 'Breakfast.'
'Breakfast,' Fred writes. He looks at the wall.
He writes, 'We eat breakfast in the morning. We don't eat breakfast in the afternoon and we don't eat it at night.'
5 'No,' he says. 'That's silly. My father works at night. He eats breakfast in the afternoon.'
He writes, 'I don't eat breakfast in the afternoon, but my father does. My father eats fish for breakfast. I eat apples.'
He reads his composition. 'It's silly,' he says.
10 He writes, 'We don't eat breakfast in our house.'

GUIDED COMPOSITION

Answer these questions in one paragraph. Do not use more than 50 words.

1 Do we eat breakfast at night or not?
2 Do we eat it in the morning or in the evening?
3 What does Fred's father do at night?
4 Does he eat his breakfast in the morning or in the afternoon?
5 What does he eat?
6 Does Fred eat breakfast in the afternoon or not?
7 Does Fred eat breakfast in the morning or not?
8 What does Fred eat for breakfast?

MULTIPLE CHOICE QUESTIONS

Only one answer in each exercise is right. Choose (a), (b), (c) or (d).

1 (a) We eat breakfast in the morning.
  (b) Fred's father eats breakfast in the morning.
  (c) Fred eats fish for breakfast.
  (d) Fred eats breakfast in the afternoon.

2 (a) Fred's father eats apples.
  (b) Fred's father works in the afternoon.
  (c) Fred's father works at night.
  (d) Fred's father doesn't work at night.

3 'My father works ...... night.' (line 5)
  (a) at   (b) to   (c) in   (d) the

4 'My father eats fish ...... breakfast.' (l. 8)
  (a) to   (b) for   (c) on   (d) in

5 'I don't eat breakfast in the afternoon, but my father ......' (ll. 7–8)
  (a) does   (b) eats   (c) is eating   (d) doesn't

6 'No,' he .... 'That's silly.' (l. 5)
  (a) speaks   (b) says   (c) questions   (d) asks

7 He ...... his composition. (l. 9)
  (a) puts   (b) stands   (c) reads   (d) works

8 'We don't eat breakfast in our ....' (l. 10)
  (a) composition   (b) night   (c) house   (d) fish

SENTENCE STRUCTURE

Join these two sentences with 'and'; then check your answer against the text.

We don't eat breakfast in the afternoon. We don't eat breakfast at night.

We don't eat .... (lines 3–4)

12 Tiger is going to sea

'I'm not going to be a bus driver,' Fred says. 'I'm going to sea. I'm going to be a sailor.'

'All right,' his father says. 'One of my friends is a sailor. He's on a big ship.'

5 'Is the food good?' Fred asks.

'Yes, it is.'

'What do sailors eat?'

'They eat fish,' Bill says.

'And . . . ?'

10 'And . . . fish,' Bill says.

'Oh,' Fred says. 'Do they eat apples?'

Bill answers, 'No, they don't. They eat fish. In the morning. In the afternoon. In the evening. And at night.'

'I'm not going to be a sailor,' Fred says, 'but Tiger is.'

GUIDED COMPOSITION

Answer these questions in one paragraph. Do not use more than 50 words.

1 What is Fred going to be?
2 Is a sailor's food good or bad?
3 What does he eat?
4 Does he eat fish in the morning, in the afternoon, in the evening and at night or not?
5 Does he eat apples or not?
6 Is Fred going to be a sailor now or not?
7 Is Tiger, or not?

MULTIPLE CHOICE QUESTIONS

Only one question in each exercise is right. Choose (a), (b), (c) or (d).

1 (a) One of Fred's friends is a sailor.
  (b) Fred isn't a sailor.
  (c) One of Bill's friends isn't a sailor.
  (d) Tiger is a sailor.

2 Sailors ...
  (a) don't eat fish.
  (b) eat apples.
  (c) eat fish.
  (d) eat apples in the morning.

3 'He's ...... a big ship.' (line 4)
  (a) at   (b) from   (c) on   (d) under

4 'I'm going to be a sailor.' (l. 2)
  (a) I am a sailor.   (b) You are a sailor.
  (c) I am not a sailor.   (d) Tiger is a sailor.

5 'Do they eat apples?' (l. 11)
  (a) 'Yes, they don't.'   (b) 'No, they do.'
  (c) 'No, they aren't.'   (d) 'No, they don't.'

6 One of these is not food:
  (a) fish   (b) apples   (c) morning   (d) bread

7 'Is the food good?' Fred .... (l. 5)
  (a) asks   (b) answers   (c) speaks   (d) questions

8 1, 2, 3, 4 is right. But 4, 2, 3, 1 isn't right.
  (a) morning afternoon evening night
  (b) afternoon evening morning night
  (c) night morning evening afternoon
  (d) night evening afternoon morning

SENTENCE STRUCTURE

Join these two sentences with 'but'; then check your answer against the text.

I'm not going to be a sailor. Tiger is going to be a sailor.
I'm .... (line 14)

13 In the country

Miss Murch and Mr Jones go for a walk. They go into the country. They sit under a tree and look at the sky.
  Fred and Charley are behind the tree.
  'It's nice here,' Mr Jones says.
5 'Yes, Harold,' she answers.
  'I'm happy,' he says. 'The country is nice. The sun is nice. The grass is nice. The cows are nice.'
  'I'm happy too,' she says.
  'Yes,' he says, 'You're a teacher. Your work is nice.'
10 'Oh, Harold.'
  'And the boys and girls in your class are nice.'
  'And your apples are nice,' Fred says. 'Run, Charley!'

GUIDED COMPOSITION

Answer these questions in one paragraph. Do not use more than 55 words.

1 Do Miss Murch and Mr Jones go into the country or to the sea?
2 Do they sit in a field or under a tree?
3 Are Fred and Charley in front of the tree or behind the tree?
4 Does Mr Jones say, 'It's nice here,' or not?
5 Does he say to Miss Murch, 'The boys and girls in your class are nice,' or not?
6 Does Fred say to him, 'And your apples are nice,' or not?

MULTIPLE CHOICE QUESTIONS

Only one answer in each exercise is right. Choose (a), (b), (c) or (d).

1 'And your apples are nice,' Fred says.
   Mr Jones now says, ...
   (a) 'Thank you, Fred.'
   (b) 'Yes, they are.'
   (c) 'Go away!'
   (d) 'No, they're not.'

2 Fred says, 'Run, Charley!'
   Charley now ...
   (a) runs.
   (b) sits under a tree.
   (c) does not run.
   (d) looks at the sky.

3 They go ...... the country.   (lines 1–2)
   (a) at   (b) into   (c) to   (d) in

4 They sit ...... a tree. (l. 2)
   (a) on   (b) under   (c) down   (d) over

5 'And the boys and girls ...... your class are nice.' (l. 11)
   (a) to   (b) at   (c) into   (d) in

6 They are not behind the tree. They are ...... it.
   (a) between   (b) in front of   (c) on   (d) in

7 'Under' is the opposite of ...
   (a) up   (b) in front of   (c) beside   (d) over

8 There aren't ...... in the country.
   (a) horses   (b) roads   (c) ships   (d) birds

SENTENCE STRUCTURE

Join these two sentences with 'and'; then check your answer against the text.

They sit under a tree. They look at the sky.

They sit .... (line 2)

14 Not apples—pears

It is night. Mr Jones's mother is in bed. Mr Jones is sitting in his garden. Miss Murch is beside him.

'I'm a happy man,' Mr Jones says. 'Soon you're going to be my wife.'

5 'Yes,' Miss Murch says. 'Oh, Harold, look at the moon!'
'Yes,' he says. 'Oh!'
'What is it, Harold?'
'There's a big fat boy on the wall,' he says. 'He's coming over it.'

10 'Fred Smith,' she says.
'There are two boys now.'
'And Charley, his friend.'
'And a girl.'
'Fred's sister! And they're going to take your apples.'

15 'No, they aren't,' Mr Jones says. 'My pears.'

GUIDED COMPOSITION

Answer these questions in one paragraph. Do not use more than 50 words.

1 Is Mr Jones sitting in his room or in his garden?
2 Is Miss Murch beside him or not?
3 Is Mr Jones a sad man or a happy man?
4 Is Miss Murch going to be his wife or not?
5 Is Fred coming over the wall or not?
6 Are his sister and Charley with him or not?
7 Are they going to take Mr Jones's apples or Mr Jones's pears?

MULTIPLE CHOICE QUESTIONS

Only one answer is right in each exercise. Choose (a), (b), (c) or (d).

1 Mr Jones is happy because ...
   (a) his mother is in bed.
   (b) Fred is coming over the wall.
   (c) Miss Murch is with him.
   (d) he is eating pears.

2 (a) Two girls and a boy come over the wall.
   (b) A man, a woman and a girl come over the wall.
   (c) Two boys and a girl come over the wall.
   (d) Three boys and a girl come over the wall.

3 'Soon ...... my wife.' (lines 3–4)
   (a) you are   (b) you are being
   (c) you are going   (d) you are going to be

4 'And they're going to take your apples.' (l. 14)
   (a) 'No, they don't.'   (b) 'No, they aren't.'
   (c) 'No, not taking.'   (d) 'No, they aren't taking.'

5 '...... two boys now.' (l. 11)
   (a) We are   (b) You are   (c) There are   (d) They are

6 The moon is ...
   (a) in bed   (b) in the sky   (c) in the garden   (d) on the wall

7 'Over' is the opposite of ... (ll. 8–9)
   (a) down   (b) out   (c) behind   (d) under

8 Mr Jones's wall stands ...... his garden and the road.
   (a) behind   (b) between   (c) in front of   (d) over

SENTENCE STRUCTURE

Make a sentence from these words; then check your answer against the text.

There's on the fat big wall a boy.

There's .... (line 8)

15 Fred and new teachers

'Mildred isn't here,' Fred says.

'Mildred isn't coming,' Charley answers. 'She's Mrs Jones now. There's a new teacher now.'

'Good,' Fred says. 'I eat new teachers for breakfast.'

5 'DO YOU?' The new teacher comes into the room. 'My name is Scroogs,' he says. He is a big man. He has a big red face and big thick arms. 'What do you do to new teachers, boy?'

Fred's face is white. 'I cl . . . cl . . . clean the bla . . . blackboard for them, sir.'

10 'Good. Now come and sit here. In the front. Near me. We're going to be friends.'

'Ye . . . yes, s . . . sir.' Fred says. 'Th . . . th . . . th . . . thank you, sir.'

GUIDED COMPOSITION

Answer these questions in one paragraph. Do not use more than 50 words.
1 Is Miss Murch in the classroom or not?
2 What is she now?
3 Is there a new teacher now or not?
4 Does Fred say, 'I eat new teachers for breakfast' or not?
5 What is the new teacher's name?
6 Has he a big red face and thick arms or not?
7 Does Fred eat him or not?

MULTIPLE CHOICE QUESTIONS

Only one answer is right in each exercise. Choose (a), (b), (c) or (d).

1 Mildred...
   (a) is with Mrs Jones.
   (b) is in the classroom.
   (c) is Mrs Jones.
   (d) is a new teacher.

2 Mr Scroogs...
   (a) has a white face and thick arms.
   (b) goes and sits near Fred.
   (c) has a red face and thick arms.
   (d) cleans the blackboard.

3 'I eat new teachers for breakfast.' (line 4)
   (a) 'Eat you?'   (b) 'You eat?'   (c) 'Do you?'   (d) 'Are you eating?'

4 'What ...... to new teachers, boy?' (l. 7)
   (a) do you do   (b) are you doing   (c) do you   (d) you do

5 'I clean the blackboard ...... them, sir.' (ll. 8–9)
   (a) with   (b) on   (c) for   (d) near

6 'She's Mrs Jones now.' She's Mr Jones's ...... (ll. 2–3)
   (a) mother   (b) sister   (c) daughter   (d) wife

7 Mr Scroogs's arms are thick. They are not ...... (l. 7)
   (a) thin   (b) short   (c) tall   (d) long

8 Fred sits near Mr Scroogs. He sits ...... him. (l. 10)
   (a) beside   (b) in front of   (c) behind   (d) with

SENTENCE STRUCTURES

Join these two sentences with 'and'; then check your answer against the text.

Now come here. Now sit here.

Now .... (line 10)

LONGMAN GROUP LIMITED
London

Associated companies, branches and representatives throughout the world

© Longman Group Ltd 1971

All rights reserved. No part of this publication may be reproduced, stored in a retrieval system, or transmitted in any form or by any means—electronic, mechanical, photocopying, recording, or otherwise—without the prior permission of the Copyright owner.

*First published *1971*
*New impressions *1972; *1973; *1974; *1975*

ISBN 0 582 52294 3

Illustrated by Gordon Davey

Printed in Great Britain by
Lowe and Brydone (Printers) Ltd, Thetford, Norfolk